# Your Pastor & You

*understanding the relationship
between a Christian and his pastor*

Paul Chappell
& Cary Schmidt

Striving Together Publications
4020 E. Lancaster Blvd.
Lancaster, CA 93535
800.201.7748

Edited by Cary Schmidt
Cover design by Jeremy Lofgren
Layout by Craig Parker

ISBN 0-9726506-5-2

Printed in the United States of America

# Table of Contents

# Foreword

This booklet is written to help develop the nurturing and biblical relationship of grace between a pastor and people.

The biblical office of the pastor is often misunderstood and even despised by many in our world today. This booklet gives a biblical survey of the office of the pastor and his relationship to the congregation. It is our prayer that as you read these pages, you will understand the vital relationship that God wants you to have with a Bible-believing and Bible-preaching pastor.

Your pastor takes his ministry calling and his role as the undershepherd of your life very seriously. His responsibilities are great, and are designed by God to benefit your spiritual growth and well-being.

Your pastor needs your prayer, support, and encouragement desperately if he is to become the pastor God wants him to be.

Pastors are dropping out of the ministry and walking away from their pulpits in record numbers. Some fail morally or doctrinally. Others leave because of trials or discouragement. Still others are forced to leave by antagonistic church members or leaders.

We need good men to continue teaching, preaching, loving, and giving their lives for the spiritual health and blessing of God's people! Just as your pastor is a vital link in your spiritual growth, even so, you are a vital link in his!

So, let us dig in and begin to understand more about this valuable relationship!

# CHAPTER ONE

# The Right Relationship of Spiritual Leadership

> *Obey them that have the rule over you, and submit yourselves: for they watch for your souls, as they that must give account, that they may do it with joy, and not with grief: for that is unprofitable for you. Pray for us: for we trust we have a good conscience, in all things willing to live honestly. But I beseech you the rather to do this, that I may be restored to you the sooner.*
> —Hebrews 13:17–19

It is apparent that Satan continues to attack and undermine the relationships that Jesus Christ, Himself, has instituted. One example is the home. The home was not established by the state nor the government, but by God Himself. The Bible records the beautiful story of God creating Adam and then Eve. In the very first wedding ceremony God brought Eve to Adam, joined them together, and instituted the home. Of course, as soon as God instituted the home, Satan began to attack it, to tear it apart, and to cause division. To this very day, he is still attacking the home.

God also ordained government. The Bible speaks of government as early as Genesis 8, and the Devil continuously attacks and brings corruption in government. As a result, there is a lack of trust toward government. Satan is attacking the very authority structure in our country today, and it is a tragedy.

Besides the home and government, there is one other institution ordained by God directly— the church. The local church is not man's organization. It belongs to the Lord Jesus Christ. He began establishing the church when He called out the twelve disciples. After He gave the Holy

Spirit on the day of Pentecost, the disciples spread the Word and local churches were established throughout the known world.

There are several key aspects about the church worth noting. The church is the pillar and ground of truth (1 Timothy 3:15). The church must preach the truth to strengthen the family and to develop godly citizens. The best friend of the family and government today is a Bible-preaching church.

Just as Satan is fighting homes and governments today, he is fighting churches in a greater way than ever before. He is fighting against God's people and God's preachers, and is trying to get them to fight against one another. Satan is happy when we are sidetracked from telling others how to be saved.

The local church is vital for Christian growth and is not optional for the Christian. In fact, in Hebrews 10:25, Paul said, *"Not forsaking the assembling of ourselves together, as the manner of some is; but exhorting one another: and so much the more as you see the day approaching."* God said that all believers should be a part of a local assembly, where they can hear the preaching, have fellowship, and grow. Therefore, local churches are a key to Christian growth.

The key ingredient in church growth spiritually is the "water of the Word." Pastors and church leaders are given to the local church to help with growth. This is illustrated in Ephesians 4:11–12: *"And he gave some, apostles; and some, prophets; and some, evangelists; and some, pastors and teachers; For the perfecting of the saints, for the work of the ministry, for the edifying of the body of Christ:"*

A pastor is a vessel who can teach the truth to God's people. The pastor's responsibilities are to water the spiritual plants, to pull the weeds, and to keep the garden in an environment of growth.

A local church can be likened unto a group of plants. Some members try to plant their lives on the side of the road and they do not grow. Other members plant their lives in a good Bible-preaching church, where the weeds are pulled and the water is poured out. These members will grow spiritually. The local church is not something to neglect, for it is something that is vital to every Christian, and God gives leaders to the church for the purpose of helping this growth process.

The Christian growth process is much like the physical growth process. As a person develops from a baby to a teen to an adult, he will mature emotionally and socially. He will develop relationships with playmates, classmates, and family members. These relationships change throughout the maturing process.

God designed the church as a place where people work together in love and trust as they grow through the Christian life. As Satan would love to take a husband and wife and turn them against one another, he would like to do the same in every Bible-believing church in America today. His attacks can be thwarted by understanding from the Word of God the relationship between church members and the pastor.

# CHAPTER TWO

# The Remembrance of Spiritual Leadership

The first principle to understand is that members in the local church must remember spiritual leadership. In the book of Hebrews, Paul is writing to the Hebrew believers, probably around Jerusalem. He is telling them to remember their pastors and to follow their leadership. What was true for the early church is certainly true for the church today. In Hebrews 13, Paul specifically tells them three times something about their relationship with the pastor.

In verse 7 he says, *"Remember them which have the rule over you, who have spoken unto you the Word of God."* He tells them to remember or acknowledge spiritual leadership. Then in verse 17, Paul uses two words that really go against the grain of human nature. The first word is *obey.* The second word is *submit.*

Because of some hurtful pastoral ministries, a great suspicion has resulted against passages like this. Yet, just as a godly husband will model a life and a love worthy to be followed by his wife, even so as we learn from these verses a godly pastor will not need to "demand" a following. His life and loving leadership will earn the respect and following that God intends. A godly pastor will give his church family a worthy example to follow through his preaching, leadership, and life example.

As an individual Christian, you must make the choice to follow the Word of God and actually give the remembrance and support that the Bible commands regardless of your pastor's "level of perfection." You could have a perfect pastor, yet still choose to disobey the Word of God on this matter.

Verse 24 is another reference to pastoral leadership. In verse 7, he says to remember them.

In verse 17, he says to obey and to submit to them. In verse 24, he says to salute those who have the rule over you.

There is a great lesson taught here. Paul the apostle was not trying to convince the believers to follow *him* in this instance. He was trying to encourage them to follow their *local pastors*. What a powerful example for all of us in ministry! A godly man will always influence Christians to love and to encourage their pastors.

A *salute* is simply a greeting. To *remember* means to acknowledge. The great thing about this command is that everyone can do it! Every church member can greet the pastor. Simply put, you should always be on speaking terms with your pastor.

Another interesting note is that this is perhaps the first and most frequent way the Devil fights this nurturing relationship. Think about it. When you are struggling in your walk with God or with some spiritual issue, your pastor is often the last person to whom you want to talk. It is during these times in life that we try to avoid the pastor. And it is often at these times when we need this relationship the most. The Devil knows this, and that is why he fights it.

Friend, the day will come when you will need counsel, encouragement, and support from your pastor. The day will come when your children will need the same. For this reason, it is wise to commit yourself to following God's admonition to remember and to acknowledge your pastor. Pray for him, by name, in front of your children. Shake his hand, write him a note, send him an encouraging email, and lead your family to do the same. In doing so, you will be obeying the Bible, encouraging your pastor, and helping your family at the same time.

This is a man who is praying for God's best for your family. God says it is vital that you keep this relationship strong.

The Bible offers several descriptions of a spiritual leader. In verse 7, Paul is talking about those who preach the Word of God. These are the preachers Paul mentioned to Timothy in 1 Timothy 5:17, *"They who labor in the word and doctrine."* These are the ones who are to be remembered, encouraged, and followed.

This passage is not talking about dictatorship or some kind of man-centered, fleshly honor. It is simply teaching us to maintain a healthy, Christ-honoring, and open relationship with our spiritual leaders—those who teach us the Word, pray for us, and lead us to follow Christ.

According to 1 Peter 5:2–3, pastors are not to be lords over God's heritage. A spiritual leader may be defined as one who labors in the work of God, stays in the will of God, and is faithful to the Word of God.

For example, in Acts 20:28 the Bible says that the Holy Ghost appointed the pastors to be overseers in the congregation. The Holy Spirit appointed them to be the preachers and teachers. Ephesians 4:11–12 says Christ gave pastors, evangelists, and teachers to the church for the perfecting, or maturing, of the saints for the work of the ministry.

In God's structure of authority, He holds pastors accountable for how they steward that influence. God will hold your pastor responsible for the direction of your church and for how he provided spiritual oversight for your life. This actually provides a spiritual protection for God's people.

On the other hand, those in spiritual authority must be honorable and must steward that authority within the greater authority of God's Word. God's people should never follow a pastor who disqualifies himself or is not preaching the Word of God and leading others to follow Christ (1 Timothy 3).

Simply put, all spiritual leadership is a gift from God. This includes the spiritual leadership you should provide to your family, and the spiritual leadership that your pastor provides for your church.

There is a second reason to follow leadership. Spiritual leaders, pastors, and teachers will help you grow spiritually. A church member's attitude toward the pastor or teacher will effect his or her reception of the truth. It is a dangerous thing to have a heart that is not right toward spiritual authority because this will hinder your response to the Word of God when taught from that leader. I believe this is why Satan works so hard to discredit pastors today. When we reject spiritual authority, we reject the message of God's Word as well. The pastor is merely the vessel. The Word is the water that will bear fruit in your life.

One may not always understand the personality of the pastor or the teacher, but he should follow his teachings if they flow from the Word of God. Godly Christians will set up guards over their hearts toward spiritual leadership. They will not become flippant toward spiritual leadership because they realize there is a relationship there that involves the impartation of the Word of God. They want to keep their hearts sensitive toward the one who opens the Word of God Sunday morning, Sunday night, Wednesday night, across the coffee table, or in a counseling room.

Satan is doing his best to disrupt this relationship. God will always bless a church that allows spiritual leadership to lead. The best thing a church can do for its pastor is to allow him to lead from a heart that is following God. Support him when he proposes new ideas, ministry expansion, or special events. Stagnation will kill any church, and pastors with fresh vision are seemingly few and far between. When your pastor attempts to cast vision and share new ideas in reaching the lost, jump on board and watch how God will bless this attitude!

As long as what the pastor proposes is ethically, morally, and doctrinally correct, the Bible says the church is to lend a helping hand. That is what it means to remember spiritual leadership.

If God's Word is not being taught, and the members are not being fed the Word of God, the pastor is not fulfilling his responsibility to feed the flock of God over which the Holy Ghost has made him the overseer. If a Christian is in a church where he cannot follow the pastor, he is not at liberty to stop attending church altogether. He must find a church with a pastor he can follow.

Every Christian who desires to grow and to experience God's best blessings in his Christian life will say, "I want to be a member of a church, and I want a pastor who I can follow. I choose to make myself accountable and responsive to the spiritual authority that God places in my life." That is a spiritual response to biblical leadership.

Think about it. Do you remember them who have the rule over you? In what way? Have you encouraged your pastor today? Have you prayed for him? You can be sure he is enduring a spiritual battle for your life on a daily basis. Why not take a moment today to "remember" him.

Over the years our church has been involved in many building programs. It seems like Satan fights building programs as much as anything a church determines to accomplish. What a blessing it has been to have a loving church family who has prayed for and sent notes of encouragement to their pastor. These kind gestures mean more than a church member will ever know to a pastor who is stepping out by faith to do what God has called him to do.

Choose to have an excellent spirit toward your pastor—for plenty of others will choose a resentful spirit. Choose to be joyfully supportive—for plenty of others will bitterly oppose. Choose to pray for and to love—for plenty of others will choose to gossip and to resist. Choose to remember—for plenty of others will choose to forget.

Your pastor needs your prayer more than you realize. That's the message we most often miss from Hebrews 13!

# CHAPTER THREE

# The Responsibility of Spiritual Leadership

Every position of leadership has responsibilities that correspond with the position. Spiritual leadership is no exception. So, what are the God-given responsibilities of the spiritual leadership in your life? Let's discover them.

## To Watch for Your Soul

According to the Bible, the pastor is the one who must watch for the souls of the congregation. This means the pastor is a spiritual guardian. The pastor is helped by the Sunday school teachers and church staff. Church members need to recognize that. A loving call from a concerned Sunday school teacher is always the extension of a loving pastor providing spiritual oversight. Thank God that your spiritual leaders are doing their jobs in being spiritual guardians for your soul.

A legal guardian for a child must provide for, protect, and keep that child away from harmful influences or circumstances. In much the same way, the pastor is to provide the preaching of the Word of God, and to watch, according to Acts 20, for the wolves that come within to cause doctrinal disharmony or disruption to God's work. The pastor's responsibility is to provide and to protect. He is a spiritual guardian and watches for the souls of the membership. This is a very serious responsibility.

Over the years we have had people come to our church and distribute flyers with doctrinal beliefs contrary to those of our church. Other people have stated things to cause disillusionment or difficulty within the lives of new Christians. At these times, the pastor must encourage the new Christians and warn them of false doctrine.

If you have a pastor who "watches for your soul," be thankful. If you don't, find one soon. God desires to provide that kind of pastor in your life.

A loving pastor will choose to preach some strong messages. When he does he is watching for souls and taking his job as a spiritual guardian very seriously. The Bible says that a faithful undershepherd is one who provides and protects.

Ezekiel 3:17 explains the principle of being a watchman. The Lord said to Ezekiel, *"Son of man, I have made thee a watchman unto the house of Israel: therefore hear the word at my mouth, and give them warning from me."*

God is speaking to Ezekiel, the Old Testament prophet, and is giving him a job description. We need pastors who will be like the Old Testament prophets and stand up and speak the truth of the Word of God unashamedly. A watchman hears the Word of God, and then gives warning to those over whom he watches. In the Church Age the pastor studies the "warning message" from the Bible. He must study, understand, and prepare it for the people.

In Ezekiel 3:18, the Bible also says, *"When I say unto the wicked, Thou shalt surely die; and thou givest him not warning, nor speakest to warn the wicked from his wicked way, to save his life; the same wicked man shall die in his iniquity; but his blood will I require at thine hand."*

The Bible says that a watchman is to warn the wicked man. If the watchman does not warn him and a life is ruined because a watchman did not stand up and declare the truth, the watchman is held responsible. There are preachers all over America who are teaching pop-psychology at the expense of God's Word. They never preach against sin, warn God's people of danger, nor do they engage in the spiritual battle that is raging for souls.

In no uncertain terms, Ezekiel was told in verses 19 and 20, *"Yet if thou warn the wicked, and he turn not from his wickedness, nor from his wicked way, he shall die in his iniquity; but thou hast delivered thy soul. Again, when a righteous man doth turn from his righteousness, and commit iniquity, and I lay a stumbling block before him, he shall die: because thou hast not given him warning, he shall die in his sin, and his righteousness which he hath done shall not be remembered; but his blood will I require at thine hand."*

If the pastor preaches the Word and someone rejects him, at least the pastor has done his job. The pastor is commanded to preach and to declare the whole truth of God. From that point the individual listener must make the right decision.

Being a spiritual guardian and preacher of the Word of God is a serious calling with weighty responsibilities. The pastor must declare the Word of God without compromise. He must warn God's people of sin, lead them into the paths of righteousness, and be a guardian for their souls. God said to Ezekiel, "If you do not do this, I am going to hold you accountable for it."

Pastors are not divine. Pastors cannot save a person's soul. They cannot get someone to Heaven by blessing him. Your pastor cannot be a mediator between you and God. He does not have any more access to God than you have if you are a Christian. Yes, a pastor is just like any other man in his church in this sense, yet he holds an office that requires him to watch over the church family. This is a sacred, serious calling.

Often a pastor will lovingly confront someone for whom he is concerned or burdened, and that person will resent him for it; yet this is his God-given responsibility. A pastor who will obey God must approach someone who is slipping away from God or blatantly violating the Word. This is a sacred expression of pastoral love and care! It is a pastoral responsibility, as a guardian, to encourage and lovingly to nurture without lording over God's people.

Some Christians distort this love and accuse a loving pastor of being "on their case" or "interfering with their lives." But this is not the intention of a loving pastor or the response of a spiritual Christian. The spiritual Christian ought always to be thankful when the pastor or Christian brother comes to him with loving concern. Oftentimes, a pastor is resented for doing his job. Friend, I challenge you to take the right perspective on this kind of pastoral love. See it for the care, love, and protection that it truly is.

In 2 Corinthians 12:15, Paul expressed it this way: *"I will very gladly spend and be spent for you; though the more abundantly I love you, the less I be loved."* Pastors often love those who choose not to love them back—to help those who do not want help. Yet the responsibility of the spiritual leader is to watch for the souls of God's people no matter how he is treated. This is the kind of love to which Christ has called us.

Be sensitive to the challenges your pastor faces, and ask God to show you how to pray for him. The pastor is not only a soulwinner; he is to be a soul watcher.

The responsibilities of the pastor are often misunderstood by the world. In recent days, there has been a proliferation of movies and books that feature pastors or evangelists who were either dictatorial, wicked, hurtful, or just plain stupid. In fact, there are even some so-called Christian books that are critiquing what they call "legalistic pastors." These books are very critical of any pastor who names sins and distinguishes between right and wrong. These books and movies often take broad swipes at the office of the pastor or evangelist—stereotyping all spiritual leaders in this light.

I am the first to understand that there are individual circumstances where pastors have abused authority, hurt people, and veered far away from God's intended course. Yet, God has gifted our nation with thousands of pastors who walk worthily and serve faithfully before God and His people. Rather than cause doubt in the minds of so many people about the office of the pastor, we ought to encourage the office once again.

At the root, this stereotyping is a rebellion against God's authority. This resentment or jealousy of authority will often creep into Christian hearts and churches in the form of blatant disloyalty and disrespect.

In his book *Antagonists in the Church* (Augsburg Publishing House, Minneapolis: MN, 1988), Kenneth C. Haugk says, "Antagonists choose not to live out the love of Christ. Strife is introduced in love's place and with strife go jealousy and anger. Visible expressions of the unconditional love of Christ are among the first casualties of active antagonism."

Certainly there are bad pastors, just like there are bad attorneys and doctors. There are such in every denomination. Yet, God desires for every Christian to find a godly pastor and to develop a right relationship under his spiritual authority.

Pastors are charged to provide leadership, and so long as that leadership is Bible-based, church members are charged to support that leadership. The responsibility of a leader is to watch for souls. Many people are afraid the pastor will get involved in their personal lives. Think about it, friend. A loving pastor cannot just watch a soul drift away from God and think nothing about it. Someone who can do this is not a pastor at all, but rather a hireling. Seeing someone drift away from God will always grieve the heart of a loving pastor. It is the hireling who does not care for the flock, but merely cares for his retirement or salary.

## To Give Account

Hebrews 13:17 also says, *"For they watch for your souls as they that must give account."* The pastor's second responsibility is to give an account for the church one day. That is not an easy thing to comprehend, but the pastor will give an account to Jesus Christ for the way he watched over the flock at your church.

Your pastor is going to give an account personally for your church. This is the highest accountability anyone can have. Surely every Christian will give account to God for his own life, but consider for a moment if you had to give account for your whole church. That is a very serious consideration indeed!

I have met people over the years who get overly concerned with "who the pastor is accountable to." Oddly, these same people usually want no accountability for themselves. They worry about the pastor's accountability; meanwhile, they have stopped attending church, tithing, and doing the basic things that God has commanded. Often these people have an authority problem and desire control. They want the pastor to be under their thumbs, but do not want to be under anyone else's loving, watchful eye. It is wrong to demand accountability from the pastor and yet resist being accountable ourselves.

In 1 Corinthians 3, the Bible says that each Christian will give an account to Christ. Every believer will give an account, not for his sin, but for his life as lived for Jesus Christ. You will one day be rewarded according to your faithfulness to the Lord.

In the same way, a pastor must bear responsibility for the church. He will answer for things like what was taught in the Sunday school, what the music ministry sang and who sang, what the youth ministry did for activities and what was taught to the teens. If your pastor seems overly concerned about these things, he is simply doing what God has commanded. This is what it means to watch for the souls and to one day give an account.

Wise pastors will always interview or have a leader interview those who are interested in membership or leadership in the church. A wise pastor will talk to someone about doctrine, his personal testimony, and his love for the Lord.

A pastor's convictions will be challenged quite often. He will be tempted and pressured to bend. A pastor does not want to stand before the Lord one day and say, "Lord, you know we had a lot of different faiths in that church. Some of it I did not feel very good about, but some of those guys gave a lot of money, so I just sort of bent for them."

Hebrews 13:17 says, *"They must give an account, that they may do it with joy."* A spiritual pastor desires to stand before the Lord one day with a happy heart and a clear conscience about the church. He earnestly desires to be able to give an account with joy!

In 1 Thessalonians 2:19, Paul said, *"For what is our hope or joy or crown of rejoicing? Are not even ye in the presence of our Lord Jesus Christ?"* Paul said when he got to Heaven, his joy would be the members of the church of Thessalonica.

In light of this, it does not really matter how many radio stations a pastor is on or how many books he writes. What will matter in that moment is the people who were saved and those who grew up in the Lord under that leadership.

The end of Hebrews 13:17 says, *"That they may do it with joy and not with grief, for that is unprofitable for you."* If your pastor does his best to preach the Bible, as the Holy Spirit would have him to preach, and if he preaches straight doctrine and the people do not obey—the Bible says this is unprofitable for them. One of your goals as a Christian should be to one day stand before Christ knowing you took every message you heard from the Bible and applied it to your heart.

The responsibilities of a pastor—watching for your soul and giving account to Christ—are massive. If you have a pastor who understands these responsibilities and accepts them with gravity and love, then thank God. Choose to accept, understand, and even appreciate your pastor's carrying out of his responsibilities—even when it causes you a little discomfort or uneasiness. Choose to see his watchcare as love and choose to thrive in God's grace under his spiritual and biblical oversight. The Bible says in Proverbs 15:32–33, *"He that refuseth instruction despiseth his own soul: but he that heareth reproof getteth understanding. The fear of the LORD is the instruction of wisdom; and before honour is humility."*

As a pastor, I have chosen to make myself accountable to a brother in Christ in our local church, as well as to several godly pastor friends. When a man of God in our church comes to me with some thoughtful words, or when a pastor friend in my life, who gives me counsel and guidance, expresses some caution or concern, it is no light matter to me. I try to take these matters into consideration before we move ahead with a given project or direction in my life, until there is peace on the parts of those from whom I have sought counsel.

If you will follow godly watchcare, you can anticipate that God will bless you with spiritual fruit, dynamic growth, and a joyful heart. He always honors those who honor His plan.

# CHAPTER FOUR

# The Request from Spiritual Leadership

A spiritual leader will also be honest enough to make requests of those he leads. Hebrews 13:18 says, *"Pray for us: for we trust we have a good conscience, in all things willing to live honestly."* Paul, an apostle who provided pastoral leadership, said, *"Pray for us."* He told them not only to follow and to obey spiritual leadership, but to pray for spiritual leadership. Paul made this same request throughout the epistles.

The apostle was saying, "Look, we're only human—we can fail, or become discouraged; we are not sufficient of ourselves, and we need your prayer and support as we watch for the souls of men and fight spiritual battles." The pastorate is a spiritual battle, and Christians must use their spiritual weapons to sustain and to support their pastors in the works in which God has placed them.

If the church has 1,000 members, the pastor must watch over 1,000 people who get sick, upset, hurt, and endure trials and afflictions. Along with this, every person in the church family is at a different point of spiritual growth. Regardless of additional staff to help with the care of the church, the ultimate responsibility still rests on the pastor.

When Paul mentions a "good conscience" in this verse, he is challenging a pastor to live and to conduct his ministry with a pure and godly life. From this point, a pastor can ask for prayer and support with a clear conscience before God.

In verse 19, he says, *"But I beseech you the rather to do this, that I may be restored to you the sooner."* Paul believed in getting prayers answered. He believed that it was worthy for them to pray for him and he said, "I want you to pray, so I can get with you quicker." He believed that if they prayed, God would allow him to be restored to them sooner. Prayer for spiritual leadership is a duty and tremendous responsibility for the believer, and every godly pastor is right to ask for prayer!

Matthew 7:7 promises, *"Ask, and it shall be given you; seek, and ye shall find; knock, and it shall be opened unto you."* God is still in the business of answering prayer, and your pastor desperately needs prayer, just as the Apostle Paul needed prayer. Friend, I urge you to add your pastor to your daily prayer list, and to bring his name before God every time the Lord puts him on your mind. That might be the very moment when he needs your prayer the most.

Recently, my wife and I were visiting one of the dear members of our church. Her name was Donell Williams. Mrs. Williams was a young mother battling leukemia. As Terrie and I spent some time with her, we told her that we loved her and had been praying for her. Ironically, she told us that she had been praying for us several times a day.

Although some weeks later the Lord chose to call Mrs. Williams home to be with Him, I will never forget the fact that one of our church members chose to remember us in prayer during her time of affliction. What a godly example she set for all of us to remember!

As the apostle was closing out the book to the Hebrews, he knew there would be many challenges to the young faith of these Christians. He also knew the preachers would be the ones who would address those challenges. He knew that when the problems came, the preachers would stand, open the Bible, and speak about those problems. God told the Hebrews, "Do not forsake the assembling of yourselves, and do not forget to listen, to submit to, and to acknowledge these men as they give you leadership. They are appointed to lead you through those spiritually challenging times."

If it was difficult to go through the Christian life in the first century, how much more difficult is it today? If there has ever been a time for godly pastors and Christians to join together in getting answers from the Word of God, it is today.

The primary request that the spiritual leadership made in God's Word was simply three words: "pray for us." These three words say so much. They say, "We need you. We need God. We need something far beyond ourselves to get this job done. We are weak, frail, and could easily quit or fall away without your prayer."

Sometimes it seems that all the powers of hell are hurled against those in spiritual leadership. The battle is often uncertain, weary, and just plain hard. So, the request: "pray for us."

Will you?

# Conclusion

We see the Scriptures are clear in their teaching to remember spiritual leadership. In a day when many are forgetful of the vital role that spiritual leaders share in our lives, may we choose to remember—to acknowledge. May you take an active role in your relationship with your pastor. Go the extra step to greet him and to encourage him. Make the first move to write, to uplift, and to edify the man who watches for your soul.

Allow him to lead you toward God and away from sin. Treasure this relationship and allow it to develop your faith and your walk with Christ.

Don't let a past failed relationship with some person of authority keep you from a positive relationship with your pastor.

Secondly, we have seen the responsibility of spiritual leadership—to watch for your soul and to give account one day to God. These are weighty responsibilities that every pastor should take soberly and every church member should embrace and accept. May God give you wisdom to see your pastor's loving oversight as just that— love, care, and spiritual protection. May you choose not to resist or resent spiritual authority, for truly, it is God's gift to you.

Finally, we have seen the request of spiritual leadership—pray for us. We need you. We cannot do this alone. We need you and we need God. In this daily battle, there is a divine sustenance that can be found through the prayers of God's people for us.

May you begin praying for your pastor as never before. May you bring his name to God every day. Pray for strength, wisdom, protection from temptation, and power in preaching. Pray for his family, ministry, counseling, and the decisions he must make. Pray that God will put a

divine hedge of protection about him and a heart
of wisdom within.

In nearly twenty years of pastoring, I have
been greatly blessed with a church family who
understands the relationship that God desires
for us to have as a pastor and people. Sure, the
years have held some disappointments. There
have been people who hurt, accused, turned
their backs, and even slandered me. There
have been times of rejection, discouragement,
and misunderstanding. But far greater are the
blessings, prayers, support, friendships, and the
shared vision that God has given to those who
have truly understood our relationship.

A vast majority of our young church family
has simply stood behind me and allowed me to
grow from a young pastor into a "not-as-young"
pastor. They have responded to the Word of God,
remembered me and my family, and extended
grace to me when I simply needed to "grow in
grace."

While those "grow in grace" moments are
far more in number than I care to rehearse, I
thank God for those many mature members of

our flock who were patiently supportive, actively encouraging, and spiritually gracious.

I cannot number the times I have received an encouraging letter that I truly needed, a firm handshake that lifted my spirit, a supporting prayer that sustained me in a trial, or a word fitly spoken in a trying time. I cannot express the deep gratitude I have for a church that allows me to capture God's vision and to lead our church forward by faith.

They have listened, even when the sermon was boring. They have responded to truth, when I thought I communicated it poorly. They have given to projects they did not see and captured a vision that has taken us all into uncharted territory—together. They have united behind the purpose of God for our church, and they have begun to kick a dent in the spiritual history of our community.

They have prayed for me faithfully. They have remembered me consistently. They have followed me as I strive with all of my being to follow Christ.

And, quite simply, God has blessed this relationship. The marvelous things He has done in our church and ministry have shocked us all! He has far exceeded our boldest vision, our most faith-filled dreams, and our wildest imaginations. He has changed lives by the thousands, and He has truly caused our desert region to blossom as a rose spiritually.

While there are many reasons for His blessings, I believe that one of them is that He honors the wonderful relationship that we share as pastor and people. He honors His order in our lives, and He honors His pattern for the church.

So now the challenge is yours. We have done our best to share from our hearts God's Word. Now the decision is in your hands. What will you do about "your pastor and you"?

Perhaps outside of your immediate family relationships, no relationship will be so spiritually opposed and brutally tested as your relationship with your pastor. Mark it down, the Devil wants this one! He wants it badly. If he can disconnect you from a godly pastor, he can potentially derail your entire spiritual life and future.

Expect the Devil to try to come between your pastor and you—frequently. He wants to divide you. He wants to take you from one church to another. He wants to keep you unstable, unsettled, ungrounded, and disconnected from loving, spiritual oversight.

Expect his opposition. See it for what it is. Cast down imaginations, stand on truth, and determine that you will find a godly pastor and grow within the loving role that God desires him to have in your life.

Choose to be the kind of Christian who loves, honors, supports, encourages, and prays for your pastor. Grow in God's grace under his preaching and teaching. Seek his counsel in tough decisions. Seek his encouragement through times of testing. Get to know his heart, and let him know yours. Extend grace and patience when he is less than perfect.

We all need spiritual leadership. We need biblical love from a godly mentor. God has given it to us. Now go claim it. Grow within it. Expect God's blessing through it. And remember, the Devil wants it.

Don't let him have it!

# For more information about our ministry visit:

*www.strivingtogether.com*
for helpful Christian resources

*www.dailyintheword.org*
for an encouraging word each day

*www.lancasterbaptist.org*
for information about Lancaster Baptist Church

*www.wcbc.edu*
for information about West Coast Baptist College